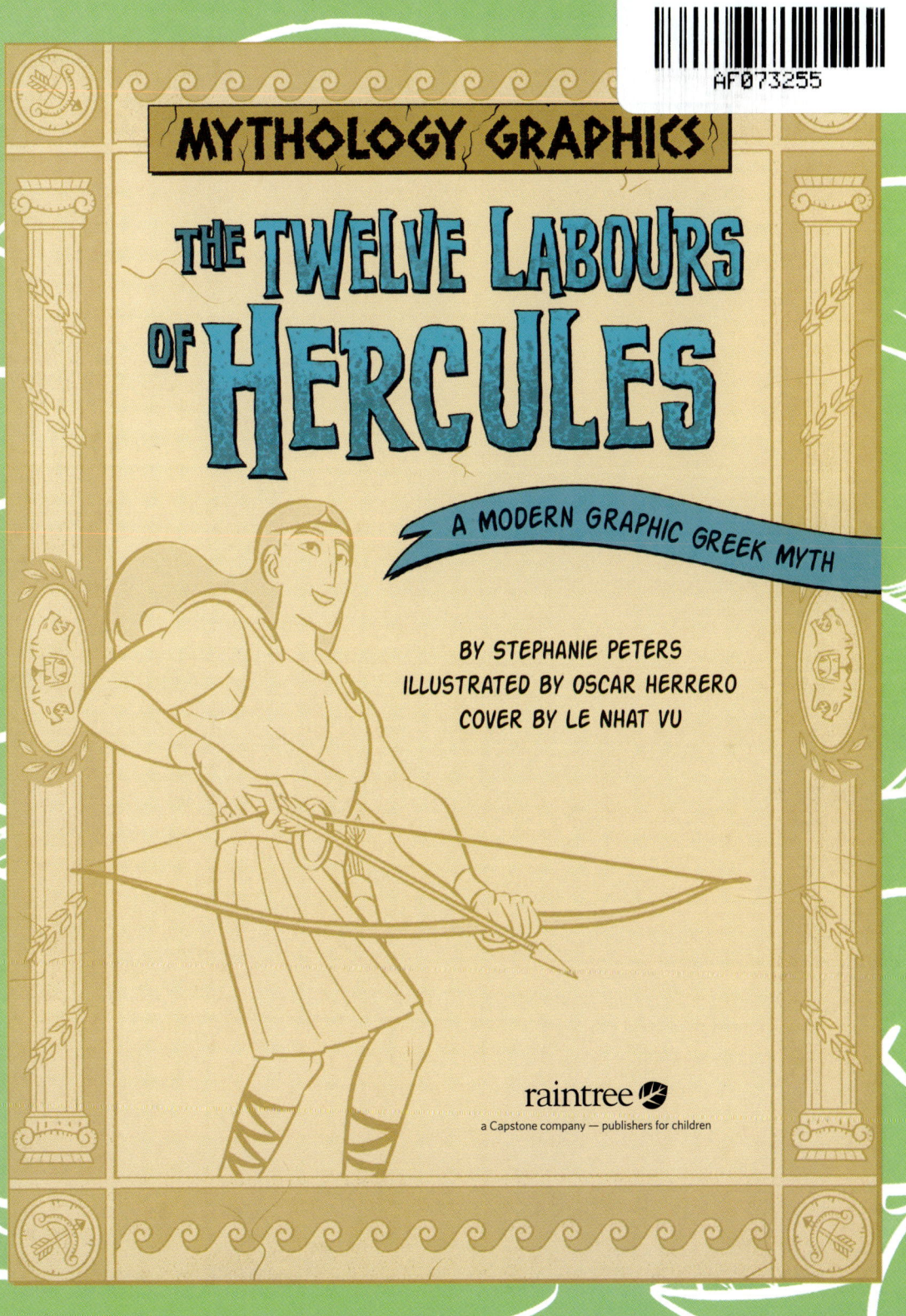

Raintree is an imprint of Capstone Global Library Limited, a company incorporated in England and Wales having its registered office at 264 Banbury Road, Oxford, OX2 7DY – Registered company number: 6695582

www.raintree.co.uk
myorders@raintree.co.uk

Text © Capstone Global Library Limited 2024
The moral rights of the proprietor have been asserted.

All rights reserved. No part of this publication may be reproduced in any form or by any means (including photocopying or storing it in any medium by electronic means and whether or not transiently or incidentally to some other use of this publication) without the written permission of the copyright owner, except in accordance with the provisions of the Copyright, Designs and Patents Act 1988 or under the terms of a licence issued by the Copyright Licensing Agency, 5th Floor, Shackleton House, 4 Battle Bridge Lane, London SE1 2HX (www.cla.co.uk). Applications for the copyright owner's written permission should be addressed to the publisher.

Edited by Alison Deering
Designed by Jaime Willems
Original illustrations © Capstone Global Library Limited 2024
Production by Whitney Schaefer
Originated by Capstone Global Library Ltd
Printed and bound in India

978 1 3982 5517 3

British Library Cataloguing in Publication Data
A full catalogue record for this book is available from the British Library.

CONTENTS

Chapter 1
Prophecies 4

Chapter 2
Ferocious, Poisonous, Lovely and Huge: The First Four Labours 12

Chapter 3
Stinky, Stabby, Snorty and Hungry: The Next Four Labours 22

Chapter 4
The Last Two Labours – Not! ..30

Chapter 5
The Last Two Labours (For Real This Time!) 36

More about Hercules 44

Glossary 46

Read more 47

About the creators 48

CHAPTER 1
PROPHECIES

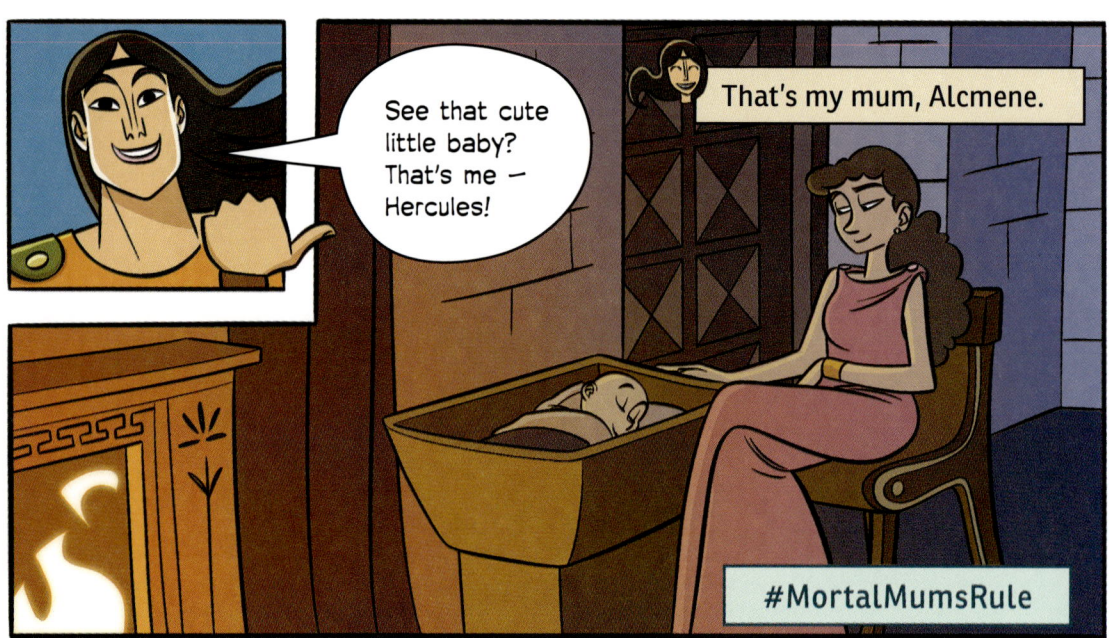

"The Oracle said I have to serve you. For ten years."

"Ten years? Oh, this is going to be fun!"

News flash: It was NOT going to be fun.

CHAPTER 2
Ferocious, Poisonous, Lovely and Huge: The First Four Labours

LABOUR #1: KILL THE NEMEAN LION

Kill a lion that's been terrorizing the kingdom? No problem.

Then again... that is one big cat!

Good thing I brought the big arrows!

Uh-oh.

BOING

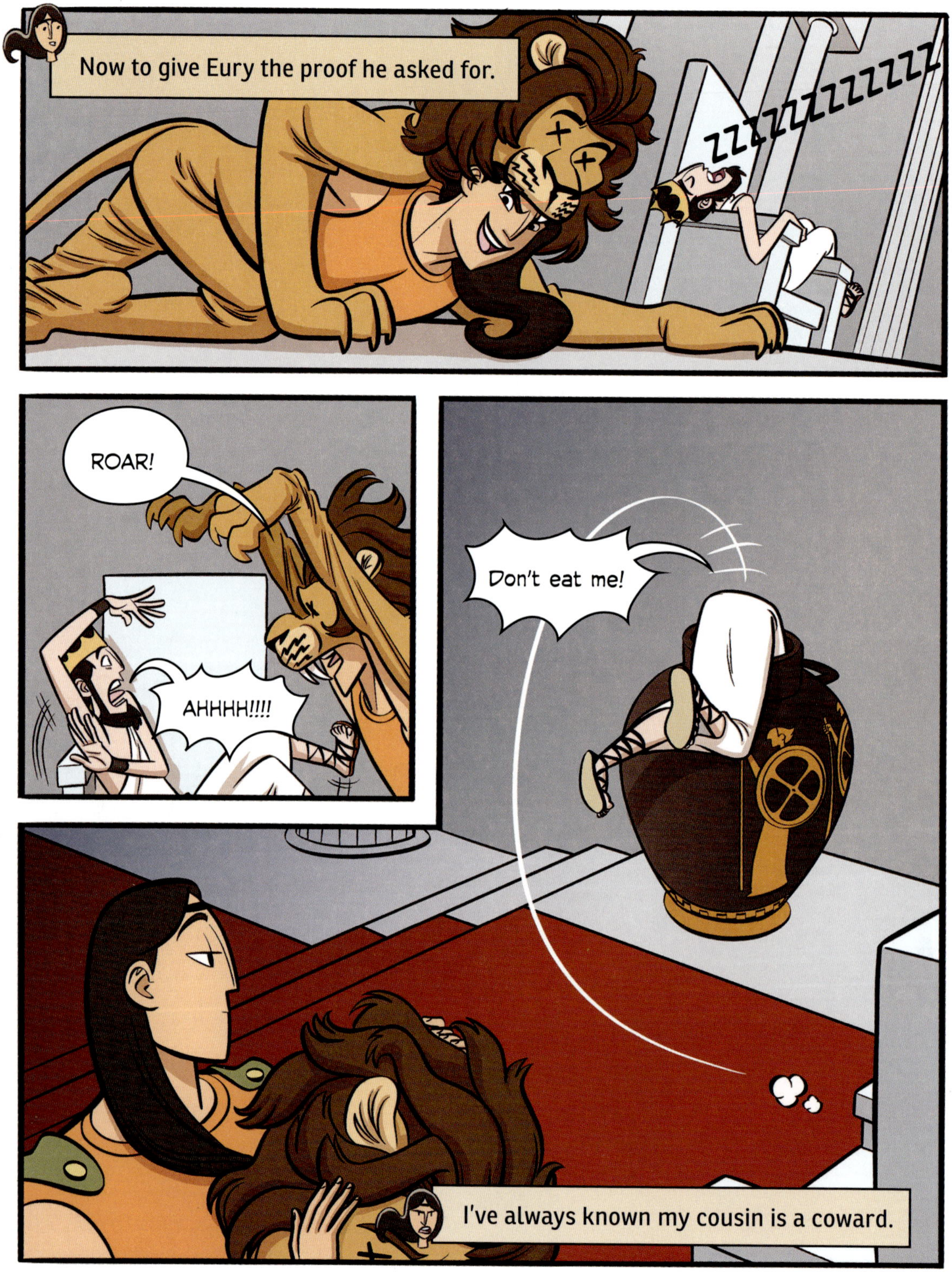

Stinky, Stabby, Snorty and Hungry: The Next Four Labours

Labour number five: Clean out King Augeas's stables in a single day.

"Your cows are gorgeous — valuable too. But these stables are gross."

"Yeah, good luck cleaning them."

"I'm a hero. No task is too big for me!"

"Wanna bet?"

#DungBucketChallenge

Nice place for a holiday, right?

Wrong. This place is full of man-eating horses.

Get too close, and they'll take a bite out of you.

The Last Two Labours — Not!

"Your nephew helped you slay the Hydra. And you got free cows for cleaning those stables."

"You owe me two more labours!"

"Nooooooo!"

Eury. Is. The. WORST!

CHAPTER 5
THE LAST TWO LABOURS (FOR REAL THIS TIME!)

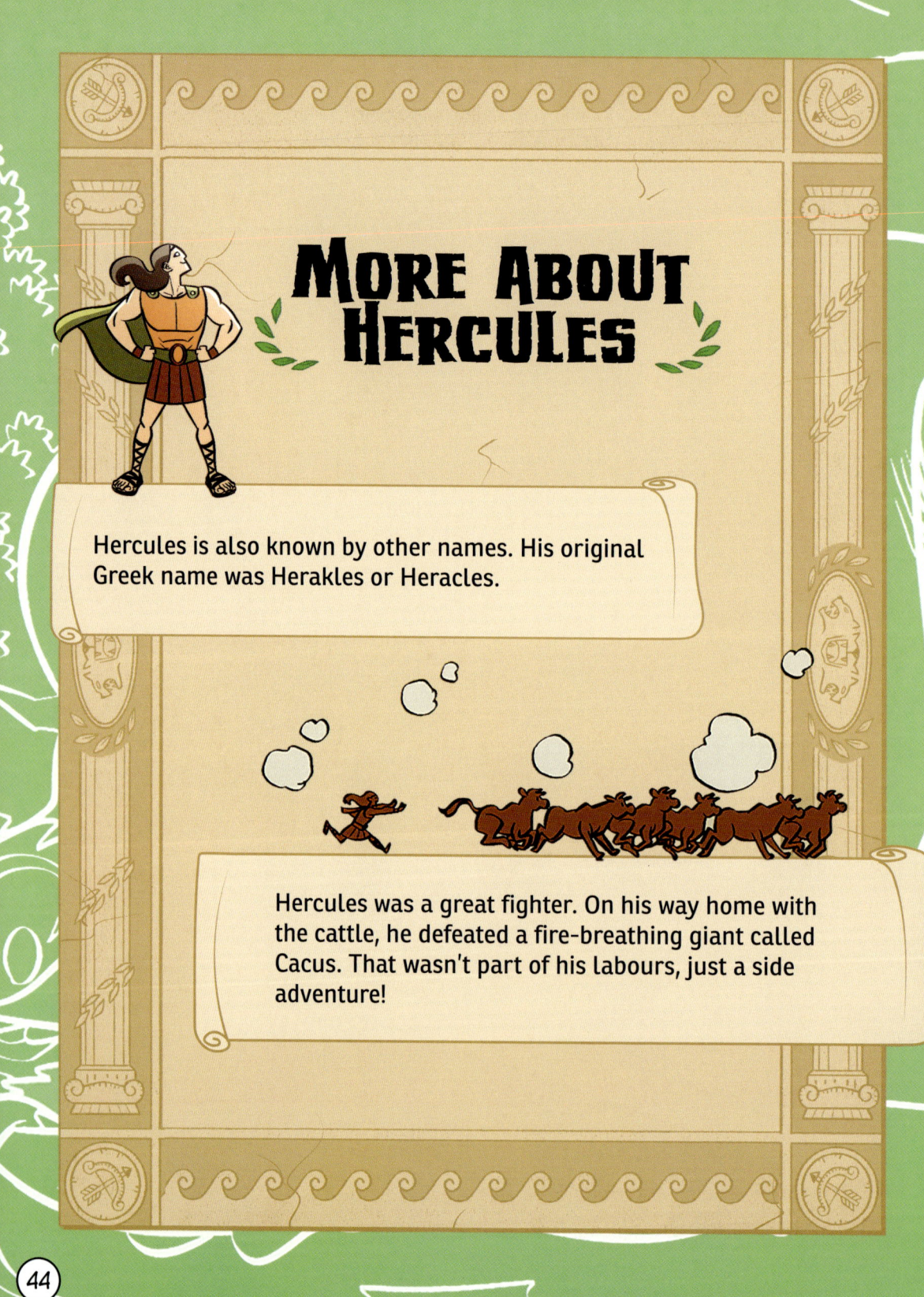

More About Hercules

Hercules is also known by other names. His original Greek name was Herakles or Heracles.

Hercules was a great fighter. On his way home with the cattle, he defeated a fire-breathing giant called Cacus. That wasn't part of his labours, just a side adventure!

Hercules was so famous that his image was featured on one of the first Roman coins ever made.

Hercules and a river god once fought to win the hand of a beautiful woman. Hercules won. That same woman almost killed Hercules by wrapping him in a robe soaked in poison! The goddess Athena saved him.

No one knows for sure if Hercules was a real man. But tales of his heroic adventures have lived on for thousands of years.

Glossary

coward person who shows shameful fear

demigod mythological being with more power than a mortal but less than a god

herd large group of animals that lives or moves together

hind female deer

labour physical or mental effort

mare adult female horse

mortal human, referring to a being who will eventually die

oracle place or person that a god speaks through; in myths, gods used oracles to predict the future or to tell people how to solve problems

proof facts or evidence that something is true

prophecy foretelling of the future

Titan one of a family of giants overthrown by the gods of ancient Greece

valuable having great use or importance

Read More

Greek Myths, Jean Menzies (DK Children, 2020)

Tales of the Greek Heroes, Roger Lancelyn Green (Puffin Classics, 2009)

Terry Deary's Best Ever Greek Legends, Terry Deary (Scholastic, 2014)

Usborne Illustrated Stories from the Greek Myths (Usborne, 2011)

Other Books in This Series

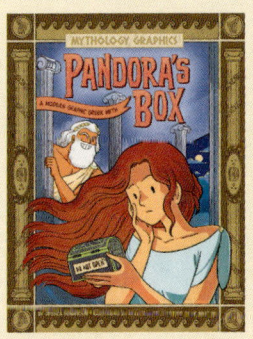
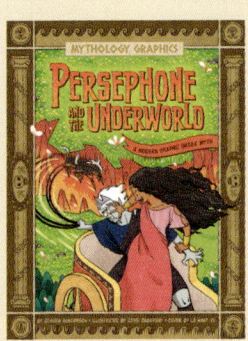
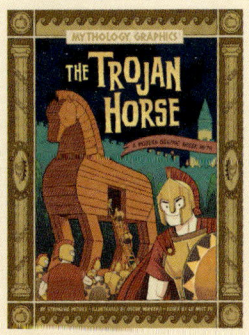

About the Creators

Stephanie Peters has been writing books for children for more than twenty-five years. Her most recent Capstone titles include *Earth's Amazing Journey: From Pebbles to Continents* and *The Trojan Horse: A Modern Graphic Greek Myth* from the Mythology Graphics series. An avid reader, workout enthusiast and beach wanderer, Stephanie enjoys spending time with her family and their pets. She lives and works in Massachusetts, USA.
Photo Credit: Daniel Peters

Oscar Herrero was born in Madrid, Spain, and studied journalism before deciding to devote himself entirely to art. He is an illustrator, character designer and writer with experience illustrating children's books, comics, magazine covers, album cover art and video games, as well as working as a visual development artist for leading animation studios.
Photo Credit: Diana Herrero

Le Nhat Vu was born in Nha Trang, a seaside city in Vietnam. He now works as a book illustrator in Ho Chi Minh City. He draws inspiration from fantasy, adventure and poetic stories. During his free time, he enjoys reading Japanese comics (manga) or novels, watching football or films — maybe with a cup of milk coffee.
Photo Credit: Le Nhat Vu